PIANO • VOCAL • GUITAR

THE BEST OF Hillsong

Marty Sampson

Miriam Webster

Reuben Morgan

Darlene Zschech

D1591648

ISBN 0-634-08280-9

HAL•LEONARD®
CORPORATION
7777 W. BLUEMOUND RD. P.O. BOX 13819 MILWAUKEE, WI 53213

For all works contained herein:
Unauthorized copying, arranging, adapting, recording or public performance is an infringement of copyright.
Infringers are liable under the law.

Visit Hal Leonard Online at
www.halleonard.com

ALL THINGS ARE POSSIBLE

Words and Music by
DARLENE ZSCHECH

With excitement

Al - might - y God, ___ my Re - deem - er, my hid - ing place, ___ my safe re - fuge.

No oth - er name ___ like Je - sus, ___ no pow'r can stand ___

© 1997 Darlene Zschech and Hillsong Publishing (admin. in the U.S. and Canada by Integrity's Hosanna! Music/ASCAP)
c/o Integrity Media, Inc., 1000 Cody Road, Mobile, AL 36695
All Rights Reserved   International Copyright Secured   Used by Permission

BLESSED

Words and Music by REUBEN MORGAN
and DARLENE ZSCHECH

© 2002 Reuben Morgan, Darlene Zschech and Hillsong Publishing (admin. in the U.S. and Canada by Integrity's Hosanna! Music/ASCAP)
c/o Integrity Media, Inc., 1000 Cody Road, Mobile, AL 36695
All Rights Reserved   International Copyright Secured   Used by Permission

11

AWESOME IN THIS PLACE

Words and Music by
DAVID BILLINGTON

© 1992 Integrity's Hosanna! Music/ASCAP
c/o Integrity Media, Inc., 1000 Cody Road, Mobile, AL 36695
All Rights Reserved   International Copyright Secured   Used by Permission

EVERYDAY

Words and Music by
JOEL HOUSTON

Moderately fast

(1.) What to say, ___ Lord? It's   You who gave ___ me life, ___ and I _____
(2., 3.) Ev - 'ry day, ___ Lord, I   learn to stand ___ up - on ___ Your Word, ___

___ can't ex - plain ___ just how   much You mean ___ to me, ___ now.
___ and I pray ___ that I,   I might come ___ to know ___ You more,

That You would save ___ me, Lord!   I give all that ___ I am ___ to You, ___
that You would guide ___ me in   ev - 'ry sin - gle step ___ I take, ___ yeah. ___

© 1999 Joel Houston and Hillsong Publishing (admin. in the U.S. and Canada by Integrity's Hosanna! Music/ASCAP)
c/o Integrity Media, Inc., 1000 Cody Road, Mobile, AL 36695
All Rights Reserved   International Copyright Secured   Used by Permission

20

EAGLE'S WINGS

Words and Music by
REUBEN MORGAN

© 1998 THANKYOU MUSIC (PRS)
Admin. Worldwide excluding the UK and Europe by WORSHIPTOGETHER.COM SONGS
Admin. in the UK and Europe by KINGSWAY MUSIC
All Rights Reserved   Used by Permission

GOD IS GREAT

Words and Music by
MARTY SAMPSON

All cre - a -

- tion cries ___ to You,

© 2001 Marty Sampson and Hillsong Publishing (admin. in the U.S. and Canada by Integrity's Hosanna! Music/ASCAP)
c/o Integrity Media, Inc., 1000 Cody Road, Mobile, AL 36695
All Rights Reserved   International Copyright Secured   Used by Permission

28

GREAT IN POWER

Words and Music by
RUSSELL FRAGAR

With excitement

Praise Him, __ you heav - ens __ and all that's __ a - bove.

Praise Him, __ you an - gels __ and heav - en - ly hosts.

© 1998 Russell Fragar and Hillsong Publishing (admin. in the U.S. and Canada by Integrity's Hosanna! Music/ASCAP)
c/o Integrity Media, Inc., 1000 Cody Road, Mobile, AL 36695
All Rights Reserved   International Copyright Secured   Used by Permission

HEAR OUR PRAISES

Words and Music by
REUBEN MORGAN

May our homes ___ be filled ___ with danc - ing, ___
May our light ___ shine in ___ the dark - ness ___

may our streets ___ be filled ___ with joy, ___
as we walk ___ be - fore ___ the cross. ___

© 1998 Reuben Morgan and Hillsong Publishing (admin. in the U.S. and Canada by Integrity's Hosanna! Music/ASCAP)
c/o Integrity Media, Inc., 1000 Cody Road, Mobile, AL 36695
All Rights Reserved   International Copyright Secured   Used by Permission

Hal - le - lu - jah, ___ hal - le -

HOLY SPIRIT RAIN DOWN

Words and Music by
RUSSELL FRAGAR

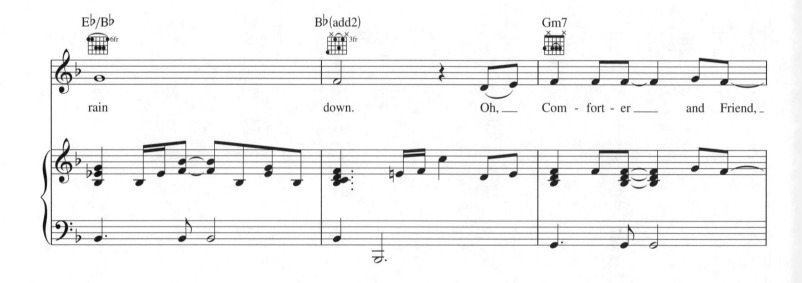

© 1997 Russell Fragar and Hillsong Publishing (admin. in the U.S. & Canada by Integrity's Hosanna! Music/ASCAP)
c/o Integrity Media, Inc., 1000 Cody Road, Mobile, AL 36695
All Rights Reserved   International Copyright Secured   Used by Permission

LOVE YOU SO MUCH

Words and Music by
RUSSELL FRAGAR

© 1996 Russell Fragar and Hillsong Publishing (admin. in the U.S. and Canada by Integrity's Hosanna! Music/ASCAP)
c/o Integrity Media, Inc., 1000 Cody Road, Mobile, AL 36695
All Rights Reserved   International Copyright Secured   Used by Permission

I GIVE YOU MY HEART

Words and Music by
REUBEN MORGAN

© 1995 Reuben Morgan and Hillsong Publishing (admin. in the U.S. and Canada by Integrity's Hosanna! Music/ASCAP)
c/o Integrity Media, Inc. 1000 Cody Road, Mobile, AL 36695
All Rights Reserved   International Copyright Secured   Used by Permission

JESUS, LOVER OF MY SOUL

Words and Music by JOHN EZZY,
DANIEL GRUL and STEPHEN McPHERSON

© 1992 John Ezzy, Daniel Grul, Stephen McPherson and Hillsong Publishing (admin. in the U.S. and Canada by Integrity's Hosanna! Music/ASCAP)
c/o Integrity Media, Inc., 1000 Cody Road, Mobile, AL 36695
All Rights Reserved   International Copyright Secured   Used by Permission

2
B♭maj7
B♭/C
G
D
til the ver - y end.
Je - sus,
lov - er of my soul;
Em
Em/D
C
Je - sus,
I will
nev - er let You go.
G
D
You've tak - en me
from the mir - y clay,
Em
Em/D
C
D7sus
set my feet up - on the Rock
and now I know:

JESUS, WHAT A BEAUTIFUL NAME

Words and Music by
TANYA RICHES

© 1995 Tanya Riches and Hillsong Publishing (admin. in the U.S. and Canada by Integrity's Hosanna! Music/ASCAP)
c/o Integrity Media, Inc., 1000 Cody Road, Mobile, AL 36695
All Rights Reserved International Copyright Secured Used by Permission

64

KING OF MAJESTY

Words and Music by
MARTY SAMPSON

* Recorded one half step lower.

© 2001 Marty Sampson and Hillsong Publishing (admin. in the U.S. and Canada by Integrity's Hosanna! Music/ASCAP)
c/o Integrity Media, Inc., 1000 Cody Road, Mobile, AL 36695
All Rights Reserved   International Copyright Secured   Used by Permission

70

72

Je - sus, You are the Sav - ior of my _____

MADE ME GLAD

Words and Music by
MIRIAM WEBSTER

I _____ will _____ bless the Lord _____ for - ev - - er. _____

© 2001 Miriam Webster and Hillsong Publishing (admin. in the U.S. and Canada by Integrity's Hosanna! Music/ASCAP)
c/o Integrity Media, Inc., 1000 Cody Road, Mobile, AL 36695
All Rights Reserved   International Copyright Secured   Used by Permission

MY REDEEMER LIVES

Words and Music by
REUBEN MORGAN

© 1998 Reuben Morgan and Hillsong Publishing (admin. in the U.S. and Canada by Integrity's Hosanna! Music/ASCAP)
c/o Integrity Media, Inc., 1000 Cody Road, Mobile, AL 36695
All Rights Reserved   International Copyright Secured   Used by Permission

You lift my bur - den _____

and I rise with You. ___ I'm danc - ing on ___ this moun-

- tain - top to see Your king - dom come. ___

D.S. al Coda
(take 2nd ending)

My Re -

CODA

MY BEST FRIEND

Words and Music by JOEL HOUSTON
and MARTY SAMPSON

© 2000 Joel Houston, Marty Sampson and Hillsong Publishing (admin. in the U.S. and Canada by Integrity's Hosanna! Music/ASCAP)
c/o Integrity Media, Inc., 1000 Cody Road, Mobile, AL 36695
All Rights Reserved   International Copyright Secured   Used by Permission

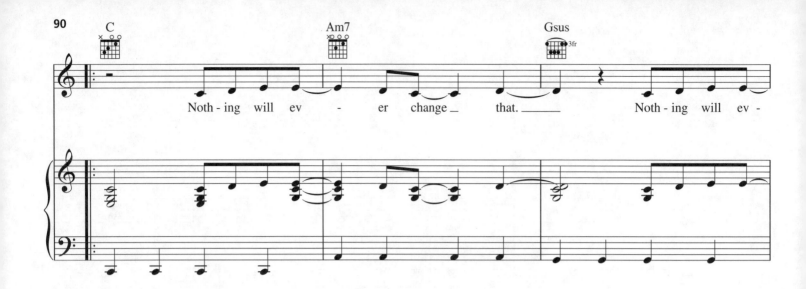

Noth - ing will ev - er change __ that. _____ Noth - ing will ev -

- er change __ that. _____ Noth - ing will ev - er change __ that. __

THE POTTER'S HAND

Words and Music by
DARLENE ZSCHECH

© 1993 Darlene Zschech and Hillsong Publishing (admin. in the U.S. and Canada by Integrity's Hosanna! Music/ASCAP)
c/o Integrity Media, Inc., 1000 Cody Road, Mobile, AL 36695
All Rights Reserved   International Copyright Secured   Used by Permission

SHOUT TO THE LORD

Words and Music by
DARLENE ZSCHECH

© 1993 Darlene Zschech and Hillsong Publishing (admin. in the U.S. and Canada by Integrity's Hosanna! Music/ASCAP)
c/o Integrity Media, Inc., 1000 Cody Road, Mobile, AL 36695
All Rights Reserved   International Copyright Secured   Used by Permission

98

SHOW ME YOUR WAYS

Words and Music by
RUSSELL FRAGAR

© 1995 Russell Fragar and Hillsong Publishing (admin. in the U.S. and Canada by Integrity's Hosanna! Music/ASCAP)
c/o Integrity Media, Inc., 1000 Cody Road, Mobile, AL 36695
All Rights Reserved   International Copyright Secured   Used by Permission

104

THIS IS HOW WE OVERCOME

Words and Music by
REUBEN MORGAN

© 1988 Reuben Morgan and Hillsong Publishing (admin. in the U.S. and Canada by Integrity's Hosanna! Music/ASCAP)
c/o Integrity Media, Inc., 1000 Cody Road, Mobile, AL 36695
All Rights Reserved   International Copyright Secured   Used by Permission

WHAT THE LORD HAS DONE IN ME

Words and Music by
REUBEN MORGAN

© 1998 Reuben Morgan and Hillsong Publishing (admin. in the U.S. and Canada by Integrity's Hosanna! Music/ASCAP)
c/o Integrity Media, Inc., 1000 Cody Road, Mobile, AL 36695
All Rights Reserved   International Copyright Secured   Used by Permission

112

WORTHY IS THE LAMB

Words and Music by
DARLENE ZSCHECH

© 2000 Darlene Zschech and Hillsong Publishing (admin. in the U.S. and Canada by Integrity's Hosanna! Music/ASCAP)
c/o Integrity Media, Inc., 1000 Cody Road, Mobile, AL 36695
All Rights Reserved   International Copyright Secured   Used by Permission

YOU ARE NEAR

Words and Music by
REUBEN MORGAN

© 1999 Reuben Morgan and Hillsong Publishing (admin. in the U.S. and Canada by Integrity's Hosanna! Music/ASCAP)
c/o Integrity Media, Inc., 1000 Cody Road, Mobile, AL 36695
All Rights Reserved   International Copyright Secured   Used by Permission

YOU ARE MY WORLD

Words and Music by
MARTY SAMPSON

My Fa-

© 2001 Marty Sampson and Hillsong Publishing (admin. in the U.S. and Canada by Integrity's Hosanna! Music/ASCAP)
c/o Integrity Media, Inc., 1000 Cody Road, Mobile, AL 36695
All Rights Reserved   International Copyright Secured   Used by Permission

126